Be Kind

By

Chris Allton

For Layla

Be Kind Kids

As a former Year Six teacher in a primary school, I found myself quoting people many times or saying something I had heard once from my Dad or a friend to "help" a child in my class. I would like to think this has had a profound effect on children in my class but I now think that reading it in a book is likely to be more beneficial to children.

The first quote on the next page is the one that started it all for me. So simple but such a powerful statement by the Dalai Lama. It was up on the walls and the windows for pupils and parents all to see. The rest are just snippets that make me think and hopefully you too.

BE KIND WHENEVER POSSIBLE. IT IS ALWAYS POSSIBLE

Find at least 15 minutes alone each day to give thanks for all you have

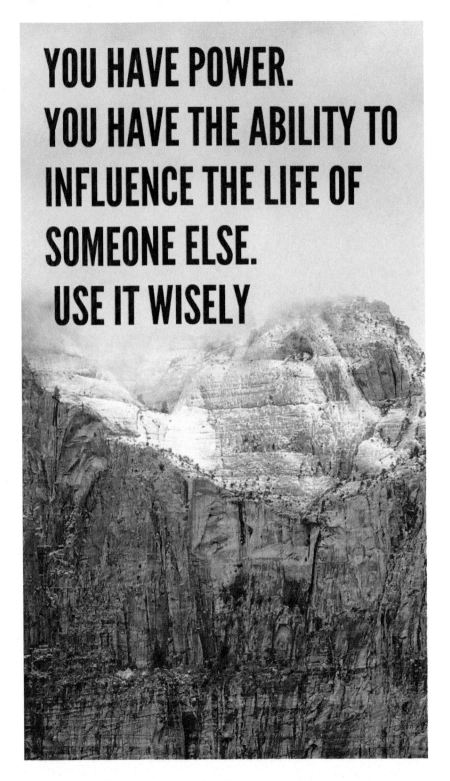

YOU HAVE POWER.
YOU HAVE THE ABILITY TO
INFLUENCE THE LIFE OF
SOMEONE ELSE.
USE IT WISELY

Recognize and understand that your talents are unique and meant to be shared

READ, WRITE AND CREATE.

TREAT OTHERS THE WAY YOU WANT TO BE TREATED.

Don't
ever give up
who you are for
someone else.

Don't ever stop learning.

Look up
at the
stars.

SUCCESS COMES
AFTER MANY FAILURES.
NEVER GIVE UP, FOR EACH
FAILURE IS A STEPPING STONE
TOWARDS SUCCESS.

It's okay to ask for help.

Always protect your
family.
(and teammates).

Write down
your dreams.
Then live
them.

STAND UP TO BULLIES. PROTECT THOSE WHO ARE BULLIED.

GIVE CREDIT.

TAKE THE BLAME.

MANNERS ARE IMPORTANT. NEVER STOP USING THEM.

DO SOMETHING KIND FOR SOMEONE ELSE THAT MAKES THEM FEEL GOOD

It's okay to cry.

Eat dinner with the new kid.

Be their friend

Never turn down a breath mint.

NEVER BE AFRAID TO ASK OUT THE BEST LOOKING PERSON IN THE ROOM.

Be *like* a duck.
Remain calm on
the surface and
paddle *like* crazy
underneath.

PUT YOUR ELECTRONIC DEVICES AWAY WHEN OUTDOORS. LOOK, LISTEN, SMELL AND FEEL YOUR SURROUNDINGS

PLAY WITH PASSION OR DON'T PLAY AT ALL

Always be honest, even if it hurts

After writing an angry text or email, read it carefully, then delete it[1]

Don't give up on a dream or idea

Be kinder than you were last week

It's ok to not be ok

(just tell someone)

Rejection will make you stronger. Learn from it

Be
an
example
for
others

DON'T
EXPECT LIFE
TO BE FAIR.
SOMETIMES
IT ISN'T.

Remember
that 80 per cent of the
success in any
situation is based on
your ability to
deal with other
people.

Wave at
people
on the bus.

COMPLIMENT THE MEAL WHEN YOU'RE A GUEST IN SOMEONE'S HOME.

BECOME SOMEONE'S HERO.

SHOW RESPECT FOR EVERYONE WHO WORKS FOR A LIVING, REGARDLESS OF HOW TRIVIAL THEIR JOB.

Keep a note pad and pencil on your bed-side table. Million-dollar ideas sometimes strike at 3 a.m.

Answer the phone with enthusiasm

and

energy

in

your

voice.

Send a lot of
Valentine cards.
Sign them,
'Someone
who thinks
you're terrific.'

ONCE IN A WHILE, TAKE THE SCENIC ROUTE ON A TRIP.

BEGIN EACH DAY WITH SOME OF YOUR FAVOURITE MUSIC.

Visit friends and relatives when they are in hospital; you need only stay a few minutes.

TAKE CHARGE OF YOUR ATTITUDE. DON'T LET SOMEONE ELSE CHOOSE IT FOR YOU.

Remember no one makes it alone. Have a grateful heart and be quick to acknowledge those who helped you.

Never
waste
an
opportunity
to tell
someone
you love
them.

Be bold and courageous. When you look back on life, you'll regret the things you didn't do more than the ones you did.

Live your life so that your epitaph could read, No Regrets

DON'T BURN BRIDGES. YOU'LL BE SURPRISED HOW MANY TIMES YOU HAVE TO CROSS THE SAME RIVER.

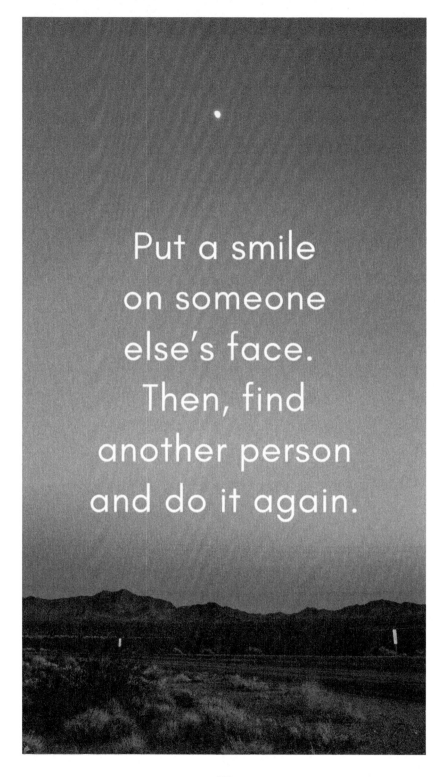

Put a smile
on someone
else's face.
Then, find
another person
and do it again.

FIND ONE THING
EVERY DAY THAT
MAKES YOU
LAUGH SO HARD
YOU LOSE YOUR
BREATH

TAKE POSITIVE THOUGHTS IN AND LET THEM GROW.

Eliminate
the
negative
thoughts
that
hold
you
back

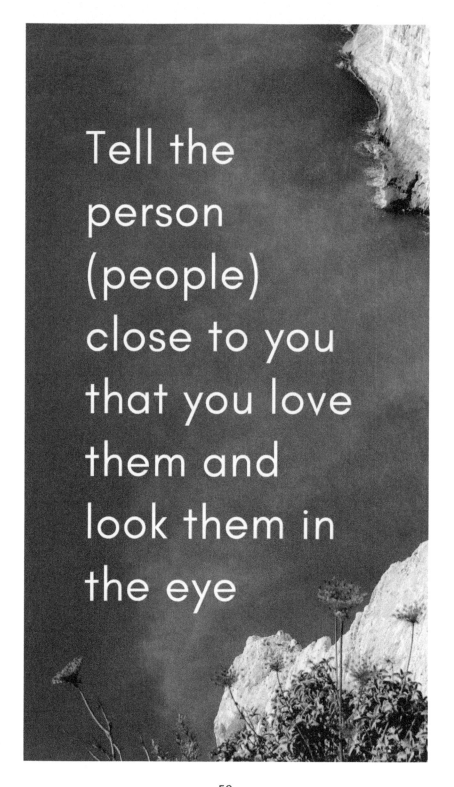

Tell the person (people) close to you that you love them and look them in the eye

Do one kind
thing
for yourself
(self–care)

SPEND 15 MINUTES READING A BOOK THAT INSPIRES YOUR CREATIVE IMAGINATION

Spend 15
minutes writing
something that you're
passionate about

Think about
the things that
have happened in
your day so far
and smile.

TAKE A DEEP BREATH. THEN, TAKE ANOTHER. DON'T HURRY THROUGH YOUR DAY

GO FOR A
RUN IN THE RAIN.
YOU WON'T
REGRET IT.

Don't
hesitate.
Act.
Magic
is
in
movement

Listen to a song that you love at MAXIMUM volume and scream out the lyrics

SPEND 15
MINUTES
EXERCISING
OR DOING
SOMETHING
PHYSICALLY
THAT
CHALLENGES
YOU

**PLAN A
HOLIDAY YOU WANT
TO GO ON**

Use less technology. Spend that extra time building relationships

Keep a notebook with you at all time and re-read the good things you are grateful for each day to lift your spirit

Live without shame. Practice virtue and joy

FROM THE FITZGERALDS

DON'T PUT A TIME LIMIT ON YOUR POTENTIAL TO DO SOMETHING GREAT

Don't worry
what other people
are doing.
Focus on you

THE NEXT
TIME YOU FIND
YOURSELF
QUICK TO
CRITICIZE
SOMEONE ELSE,
STOP.
GIVE THEM A
COMPLIMENT
INSTEAD

Beware
of
the

person
who has
nothing
to lose.

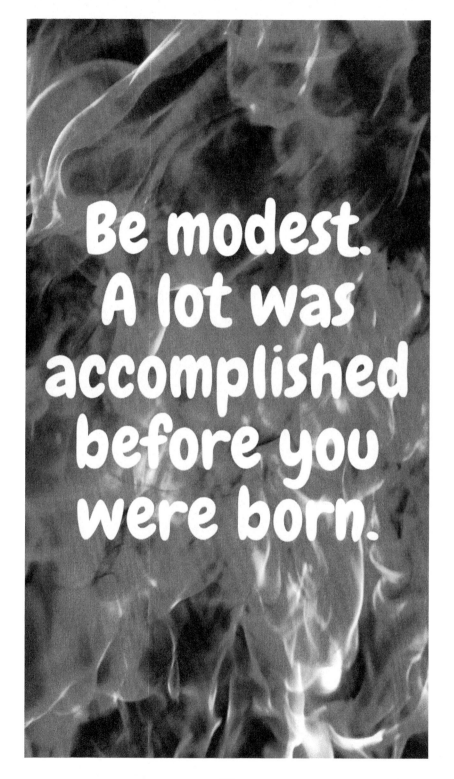

Be modest.
A lot was
accomplished
before you
were born.

When someone hugs you, let them be the first to let go.

THINK TWICE
BEFORE
BURDENING A
FRIEND WITH
A SECRET.

Be a good winner.

Don't allow the phone to interrupt important moments. It's there for our convenience, not the caller's.

LOOSEN UP.
RELAX.
EXCEPT FOR RARE LIFE-AND-DEATH MATTERS, NOTHING IS AS IMPORTANT AS IT FIRST SEEMS.

Become
the
most
positive
and
enthusiastic
person
you
know.

GIVE PEOPLE A SECOND CHANCE, BUT NOT A THIRD.

WHEN PLAYING GAMES WITH YOUNGER CHILDREN, LET THEM WIN.

NEVER DEPRIVE SOMEONE OF HOPE; IT MIGHT BE ALL THAT THEY HAVE.

Lend only those books you never care to see again.

Make it a habit to do nice things for people who will never find out.

AVOID SARCASTIC REMARKS.

Whistle. You sound happy.

Be brave.
Even if
you're not,
pretend to be.
No one can
tell the
difference.

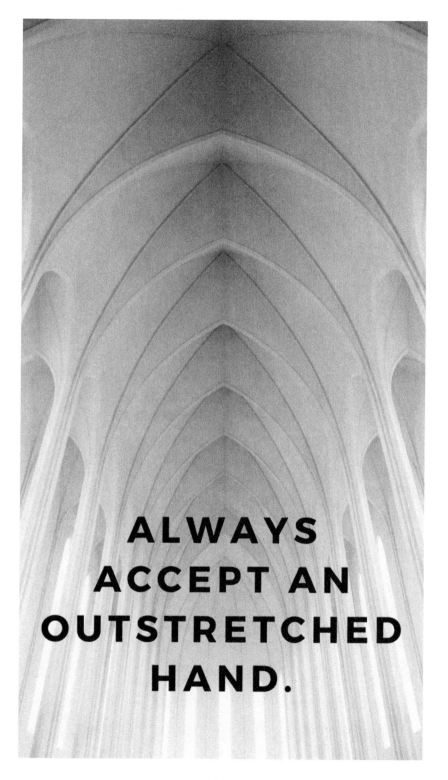

ALWAYS ACCEPT AN OUTSTRETCHED HAND.

NEVER GIVE UP ON ANYBODY. MIRACLES HAPPEN EVERYDAY.

Words win more fights than fists.

Sing in the shower.

LOOK PEOPLE IN THE EYE.

Have a firm
handshake.

Never shake
a person's hand
sitting down

GO OUT AND SEE THAT BAND WHEN YOUR FRIEND TELLS YOU TO GO. YOU WON'T REGRET IT

Don't blame yourself for past failures. Forgive yourself

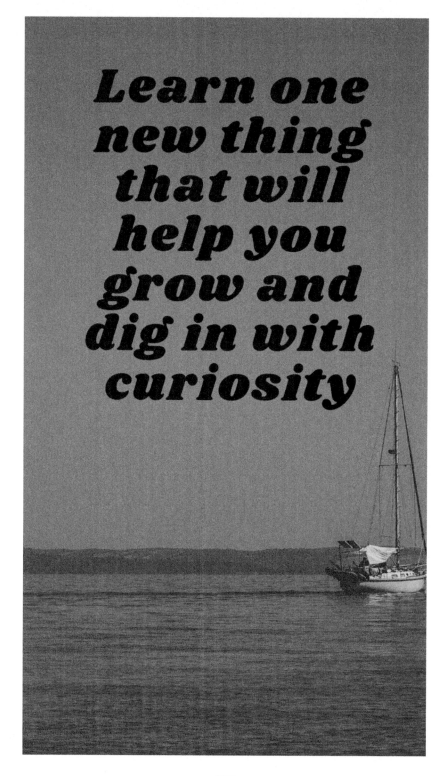

Learn one new thing that will help you grow and dig in with curiosity

Accept compliments and praise from others. Be humble.

Motivate yourself by reminding yourself of all the wonderful people and things you have in your life

JUST BECAUSE YOU GROW OLDER DOESN'T MEAN YOU HAVE TO STOP BEING A KID! PLAY, HAVE FUN, EXPLORE AND ENJOY LIFE!

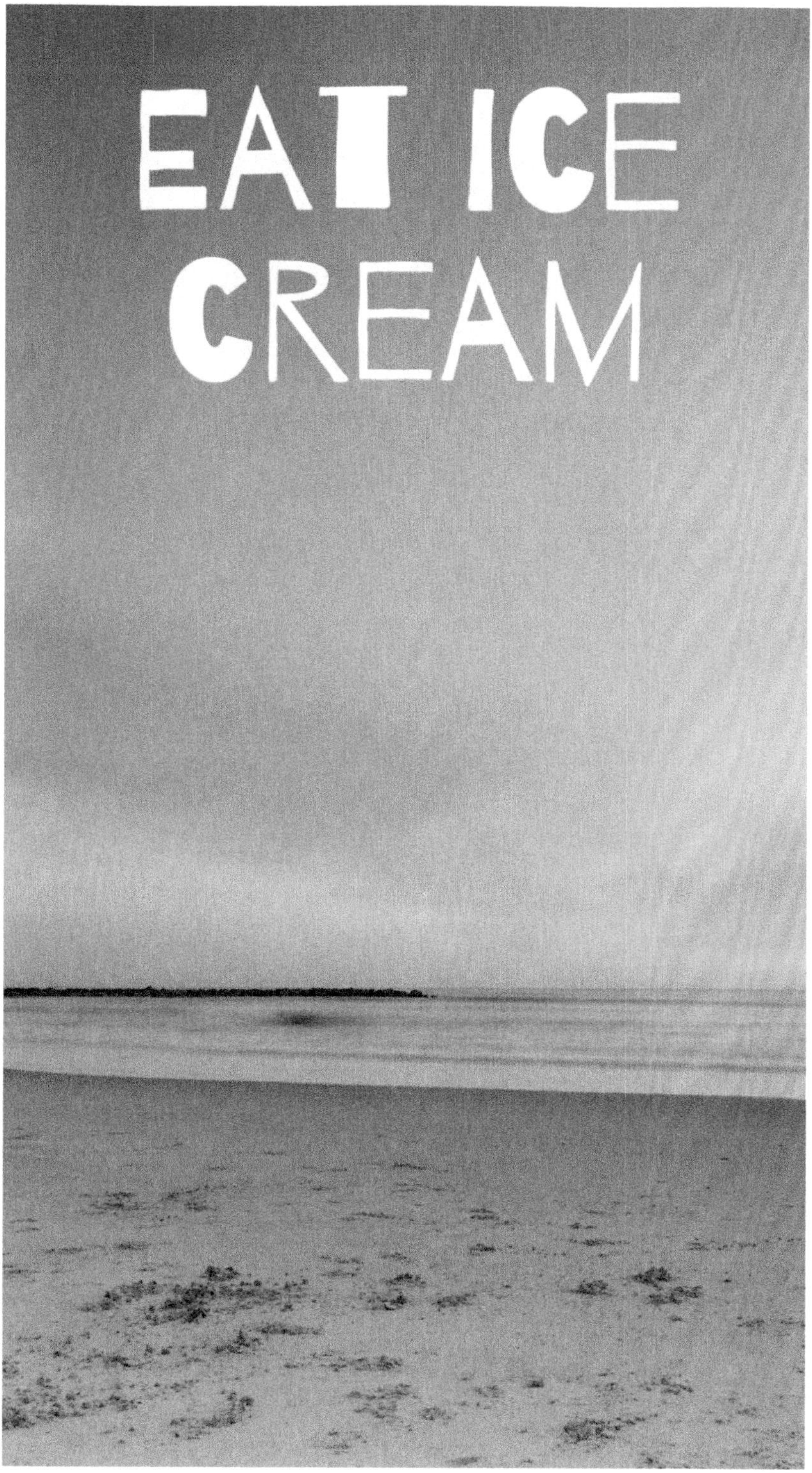
EAT ICE
CREAM

BE

YOU

www.chrisallton.co.uk

Printed in Great Britain
by Amazon